walking on the rock

avi sato

springwaterspress

for my father,

a child of the island

and my mother,

who came from afar and fell in love

preface

i was once a child of the rock, north america's eastern-most landmass, newfoundland. it may be an island but it is approximately the size of portugal so it is a vast, sparsely-populated land of wilderness, surrounded by the icy waters of the north atlantic.

inspired to capture some of its rugged cold and the vibrancy of its colors and the people who live on its harsh coastline, i have selected the spare and rigid form of the haiku, a visitor from another island nation not dissimilar in many respects.

while japanese verse may feel a world away from the salt spray and fish-devoted life of traditional newfoundland, these are two cultures of the sea bound inextricably to her waves and currents, her gifts and the sacrifices she demands of her neighbors.

journey with me across the island three lines at a time, from conception bay to the northern peninsula and back down to the west coast's whale-soaked legacy. you won't find stories here in the traditional sense but you may just smell the ocean's spray if you close your eyes and breathe deeply the essence of the atlantic.

conception bay

rocks form new beaches

as far as eyes may take me

where is all the sand

i taste the wavetops

carried on the breath of dawn

salt between my lips

flowers of the sea

deposited at my feet

what is a caplin

rowing at sunset

barely within my vision

where are you going

standing on the cliff

witness myriad islands

whose names are now lost

bells ring in the distance

calling us to pray inside

my god is outdoors

stones beneath my feet

slippery yet inviting

firelight on the beach

flames at the seaside

voices mingle with guitars

salt spray meets laughter

snowman on the beach

coated in more salt than roads

tricks the ocean plays

a secluded patch

shielded from view by the rocks

open to the sea

a house on the hill

looks down on my morning swim

in case i should sink

land of salt water

dancing with the rock faces

crumbling in their own time

who am i to judge

the ocean as sisyphus

carrying new rocks

waves kissing the shoreline

playing a game with my shoes

until i lose

did you call my name

the wind stole your voice and mine

nothing left to say

fishing in the bay

is there any fish to catch

does it matter

silent mornings

relative stillness overwhelms

i don't hear the birds

far from city noise

easy to pretend i'm alone

surrounded by life

bell island

a culture of mine

riches always lie within

bound in death's dark fires

rocks turned to fire

earth's insides becoming steam

ships moved by planet's depths

triplets floating silent

against topsail's background

an unsounded bell

the smell of freshness

mingled with salt on the breeze

and foghorns' ceaseless wail

you walked on water

as i do among the floods

on my way to church

paradise

red-painted sunsets

shiver as darkness falls quickly

yet i am safe

home is where no heart

trembles alone in sadness

who am i to cry

horizon of trees

rivers hidden at their feet

dog barks at the moon

walk between the ponds

starlight shimmers overhead

far from the houses

playing in the grass

tickled by dandelion

am i an adult

stillness of the dawn

broken by the birds above

come to visit me

pathways to cities

never walk far from my home

yet i hear nothing

above the ocean

endless waves shrink to nothing

silent miniatures

bicycles and hills

redraw the morning rush hour

as i head for home

sun above the trees

shines uniquely on my face

as it blesses you

enlightenment comes

as midday rises and falls

darkness is banished

morning shares beauty

among meters of snowdrifts

shovels stuck in ice

sliding down the bank

abandoned to gravity

until i fall off

smell of fallen snow

catches my nose as i walk

freezing words silent

stillness in the air

as if the world were frozen

until the birds wake

distant from cities

forests speak of happiness

too soon i must leave

st john's

harbor at sunrise

long since awoken in noise

where is the foghorn

towers' incongruence

party side by side with cliffs

narrow existence

ships' steel walls shadow

colorful streets with their shops

yet sunlight streams in

witness to the world

streaming through the narrow gate

water speaks volumes

yellow red blue green

children's building-block houses

suddenly alive

standing on the fort

silhouette against the sky

can you see heaven

snow overwhelms streets

new mountains grow overnight

and melt in the sun

under cover of white

the city is purified

colors gone silent

what color is home

red and green live side by side

not just for christmas

midnight on the street

music is just beginning

dancing on the deck

have you kissed a fish

questions with no right answers

lead to new friendships

lighthouse far from here

your eye blinks in the darkness

who do you see now

on the hill

battery without a phone

gazing over the city

tower with a mast

speak words into the ether

let the world echo

nighttime lights below

patterns appear and vanish

can you see letters

city built on fish

standing on a barren rock

somehow feels like home

churches of ancient stone

organs singing to heaven

land of tradition

torbay

iceberg drifting in

almost lost in the wavetops

hidden depths below

boxes on the hill

child playing with lego blocks

or are they houses

stormclouds rolling in

fear red skies in the morning

where to take shelter

field of lambs singing

soon to meet the barber's sheers

slippers in training

road on the cliff's edge

looks down on the cove below

fires in the darkness

roar above my head

far away an eagle soars

a bird of metal

lawns between the rocks

a bit of the old country

why water the grass

trees on the land's edge

daredevils cloaked in green needles

do battle with the wind

stories of pirates

hiding deep in the valleys

now long disappeared

songs of distant lands

echo against the icebergs

and lose their appeal

st mary's bay

tail in the distance

quickly approaching my boat

fish large as my house

swimming with the whale

thumbelina dancing

accompanied by giants

causeway stretching out

its hand across the water

to touch family

just off the cape

let me fish among the combers

at neptune's right hand

listen to baited trawls

glistening in the lightning

as thunder roars

let ground swells break me

as sand rolls on the beachhead

and dories run aground

placentia

dear friends speak in tongues

heard long ago in provence

alive and well here

sand between the hills

an oasis in the ocean

how does it float

cannons overlook

in their shadow am i safe

protect or attack

white fences stretch out

telling stories of times past

a simpler life lost

a yellow dory

freshly painted on the beach

calls me to its oars

silhouetted cross

ancestors stones remind me

one day i'll sleep here

coats of blue and red

castle calls from atop the hill

history alive

walls of the fortress

speak conflicts now forgotten

to today's harsh wars

clarenville

valleys sound random

fish in countless shoals arrive

siren songs of land

a bare horizon

stands its snowy sentinel

above the harbor

train whistles silent

cars resting on tracks now cropped

for what do they train

falling whiteness abounds

on freshly-departed leaves

spring can't come too soon

stand in the same stream

twice or many times today

frozen in ice and time

trinity bay

god the three in one

drew villages on a rock

a divine image

a bay of triplets

alive with the sound of jigs

living tradition

walking the isthmus

water attacks from both sides

find the middle way

jellyfish predict

three forms of tranquility

where my heart's content

house of light and sound

how many boats have you saved

from nature's embrace

floating ice castles

standing still at attention

flip in an instant

carbonear

where is lukey's boat

marvel of green seamanship

lost in the music

boats have come home

stages beyond the horizon

salt is in the air

swallow's likeness sings

a melody of flying

beyond water's grasp

rivers never dry

the lee shore captures the sun

an image of love

salt hangs in the air

nourishing the sense of hope

that comes from the sea

gander

water birds abound

calling in the morning glow

where is my mother

winged history

speaks volumes of wars' fallen dreams

hidden in the trees

serpentine waters

nourish seemingly endless trees

whose green remains

the storm's aftermath

once solid houses vanished

yet people remain

white above my head

wind gusting from the northeast

school's open today

i dream of shovels

lost in a night of snowfall

my morning workout

drumbeats in the air

metal birds spinning dancing

pausing overhead

steam rises quickly

the scent of outdoor spices

bonfire in the snow

flags and windsocks wave

inviting in their peacefulness

let your mind alight

ballads remind me

ireland is not so far

i come from away

bonavista

b'y's the boat builder

fish-catching captain of lore

who always returns home

hills crowned by sunrays

pine summers ephemeral

a new ode echoes

white cloaks spread winter

days compressed give way to stars

twinkling frozen lovesongs

shores swept by tempests

storm's fury enrages the sea

waves reflect sun's warmth

as loved our fathers

we walk the cliffs they once knew

in love with the wind

st anthony

aurora echoes

a rainbow of night's desire

sings midnight's beauty

clouds shining with blue

fade into prisms of green

as i close my eyes

facing the water

golden arm in the distance

reflects in the waves

darkness lies serene

echoing on the water

broken by the waves

the sound of a gull

awakens the town below

the fish have arrived

deer lake

dancing with glaciers

moose wander ancient pathways

where water once roamed

pond with no bottom

leaves welcome on your surface

hide the depths within

distant antlers shake

reindeer seeking santa claus

sleigh rides soon await

rocks and snow are built

by time's unsteady fingers

accumulation

swimming in the lake

morning freshness awakens

drying by the fire

hiking in the hills

ridgelines collapsed in shadow

leaves blown against my face

corner brook

city on the hill

facing the glaciers far off

frolics free of ice

crimson in the fall

fills the valley with fire

soon prepared for snow

between island peaks

roads stretch silken pathways

ants set out on journeys

fireworks from above

welcome july's beginning

a half hour early

a marble of snow

downhill laughter fights the frost

chairs head toward heaven

port aux basques

ferry departing

visible in the distance

you can leave me here

a place of returns

drawbridge to a different land

away from islands

to escape the sea

i first must cross its reaches

and walk on water

whistles break the dawn

endlessly arrive depart

the ship knows the way

gateway to a world

foreign in all but its name

sing o Canada

grand bank

where have the fish gone

once spoken of by baskets

forever hidden

spout in the distance

its body dwarfing my boat

i smile at the whale

walk atop the fish

from boat to boat with dry feet

nature's salty dance

the storm frightens me

its anger untamable

and my boat so small

waves caress the hull

last night's crimson departed

a new day begins

About the Author

Avi is a teacher and writer, one who desires to live outside the boundaries of a society lost to the artifice of equality trampled by misogyny, racism, and sexualized oppression, one who lives apart from the constructions of gender identity while crying for the necessity of that existence being apart from a world in fragments because of its unwillingness to shed its traditional attachment to manufactured roles. They have lived and studied between Canada's east and west coasts, composing poetry on the shores of the Atlantic and pacific, holding dear within the heart the solitude that comes from standing at the edge of land with feet no longer willing to turn back toward humanity's lost humanity.

They are a proponent of art as an unrelenting walk along the pathway of beauty where ideas and thoughts and reality and existence take secondary role to language as a conduit for the simple pleasure of words living for their capacity to take the listener, the reader, even the writer to new worlds deep not in their knowledge but in their pure escape into beauty itself.

hold yourself gently resting your body
tasting this moment with each smiled breath
know the peace from within
so you too may touch the nature that surrounds you
with the gentleness you have found within

www.ingramcontent.com/pod-product-compliance
Lightning Source LLC
Chambersburg PA
CBHW032019050726
47590CB00006B/2237